Milet Picture Dictionary

Milet Publishing Ltd
6 North End Parade
London W14 OSJ
England
Email info@milet.com
Website www.milet.com

First published by Milet Publishing Ltd in 2003

Text © Sedat Turhan 2003
Illustrations © Sally Hagin 2003
© Milet Publishing Ltd 2003

ISBN 1840593466

Printed in Belgium

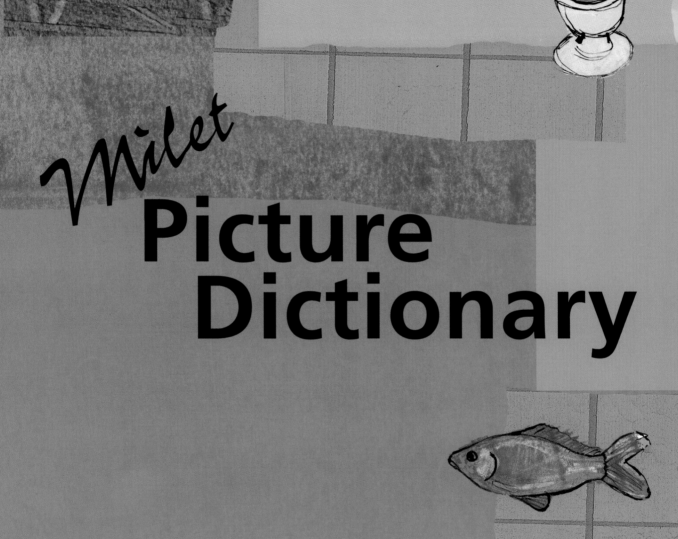

Milet Picture Dictionary

Text by **Sedat Turhan**

Illustrations by **Sally Hagin**

COLOURS/COLORS

red orange yellow green blue

purple grey pink black white

PLANTS

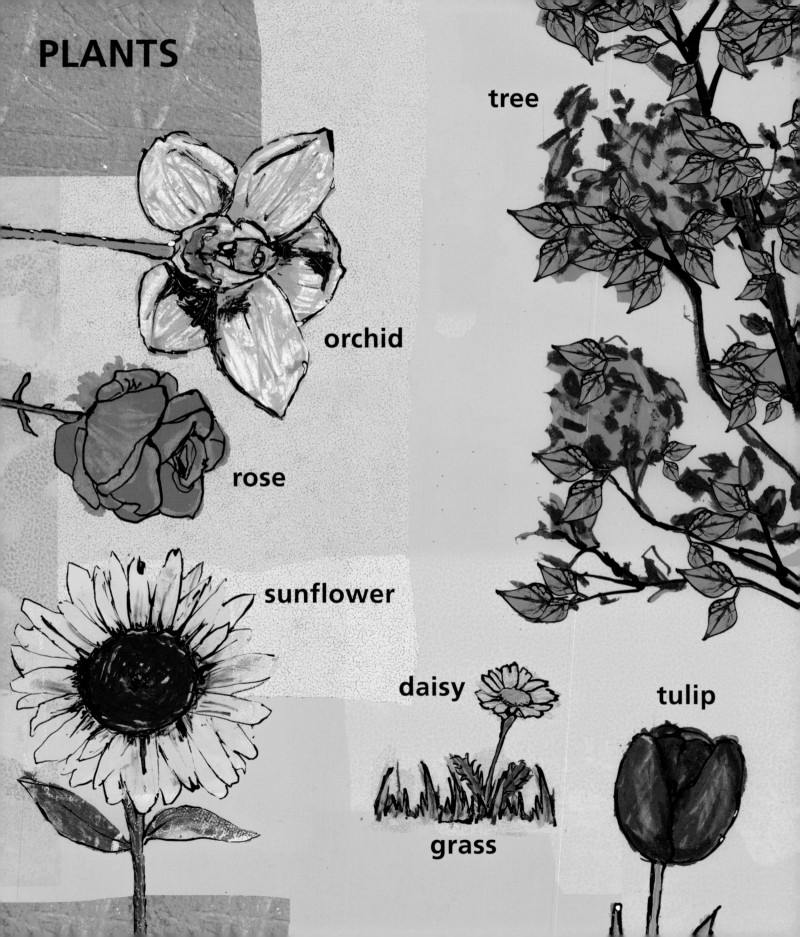

tree

orchid

rose

sunflower

daisy

tulip

grass

lily

daffodil

branch

leaf

watering can

cactus

plant pot

FRUIT

cherry

kiwi

apricot

pear

fig

peach

strawberry

banana

mango

orange

apple

blueberry

lemon

grapes

avocado

raspberry

grapefruit

pineapple

ANIMALS

lion

zebra

tiger

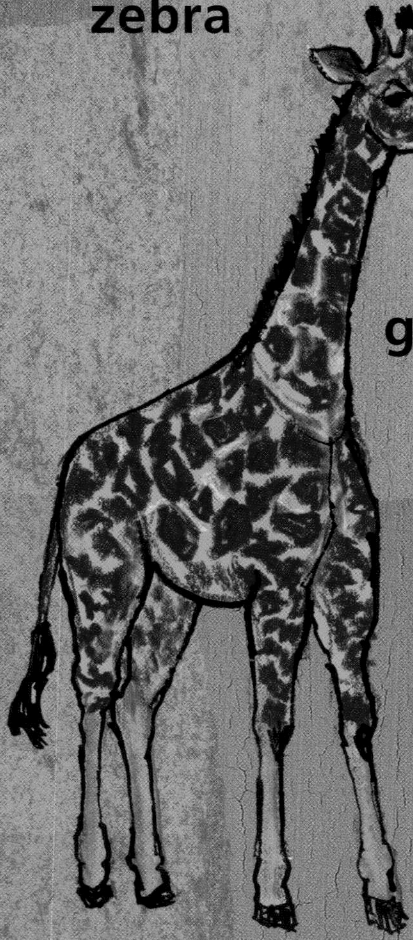

giraffe

elephant

penguin

duck

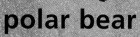

polar bear

cow

rooster

sheep

goat

horse

ANIMALS & INSECTS

bird

dog

cat

rabbit

frog

crab

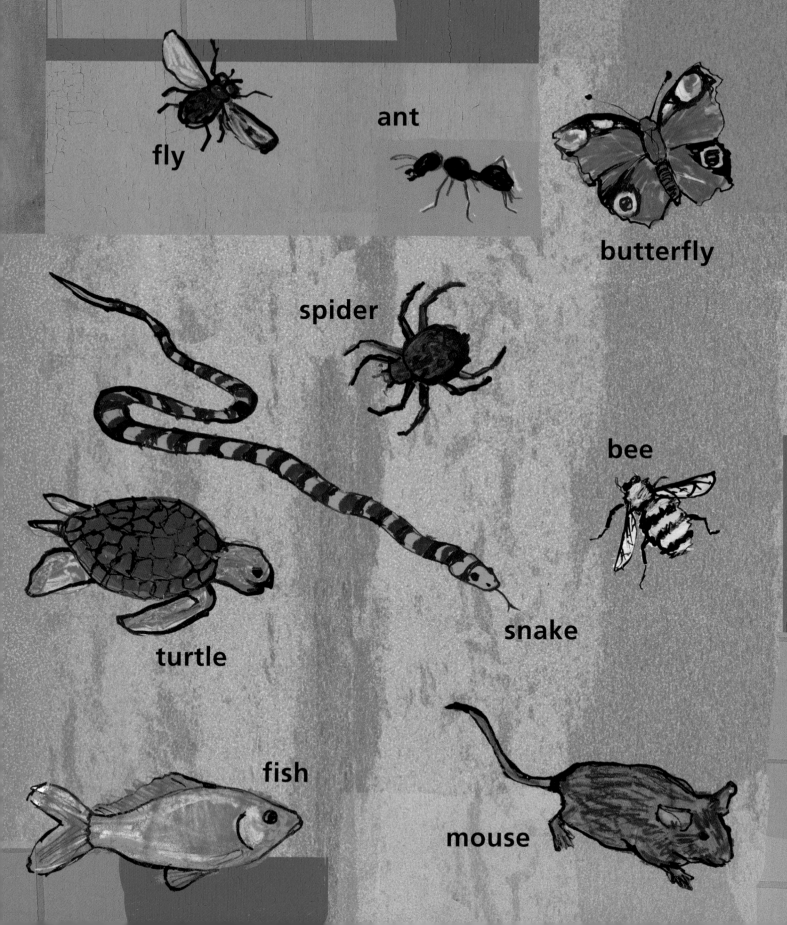

fly

ant

butterfly

spider

bee

turtle

snake

fish

mouse

HUMAN BODY

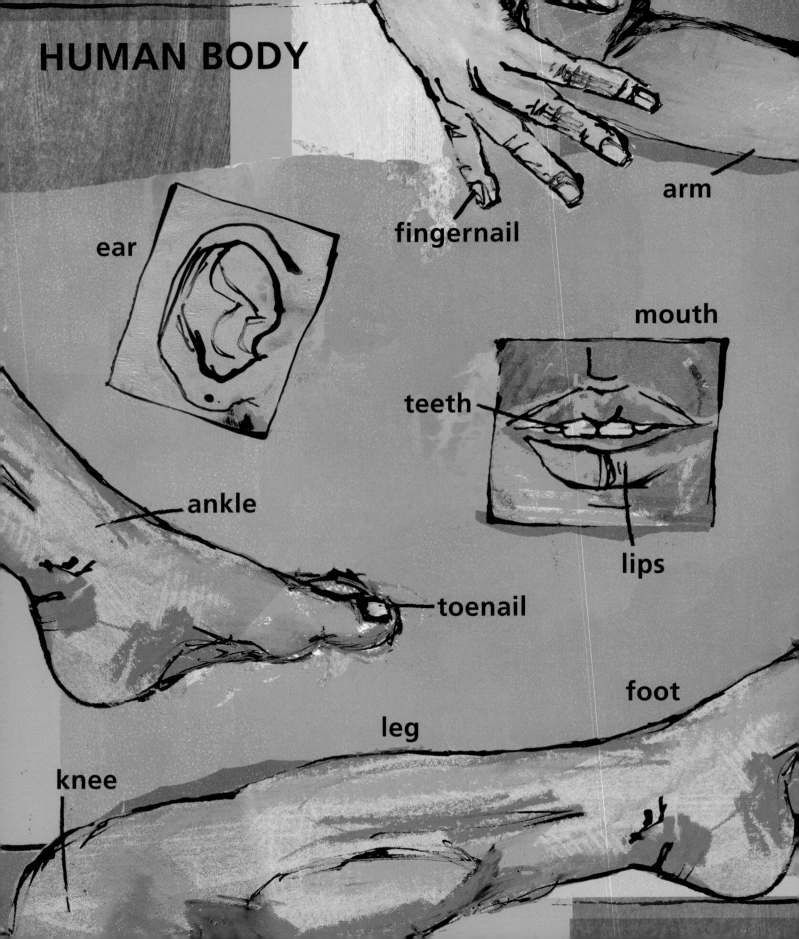

arm

fingernail

ear

mouth

teeth

ankle

lips

toenail

foot

leg

knee

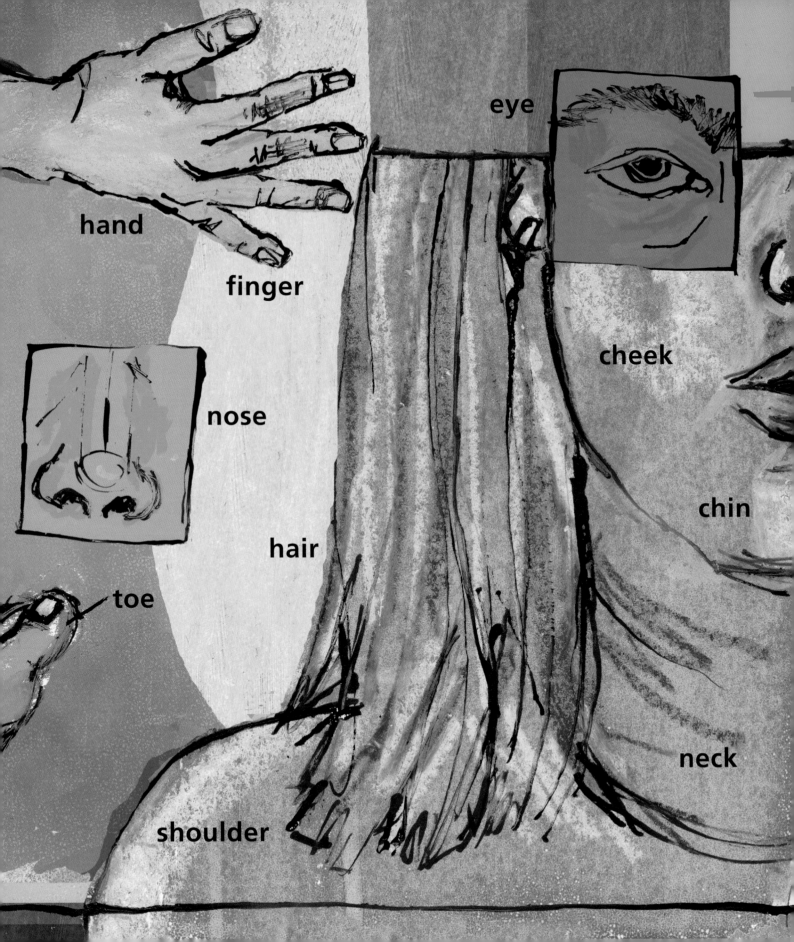

hand

finger

eye

cheek

nose

chin

hair

toe

neck

shoulder

HOUSE & LIVING ROOM

roof

chimney

house

door

key

light bulb

candle

armchair

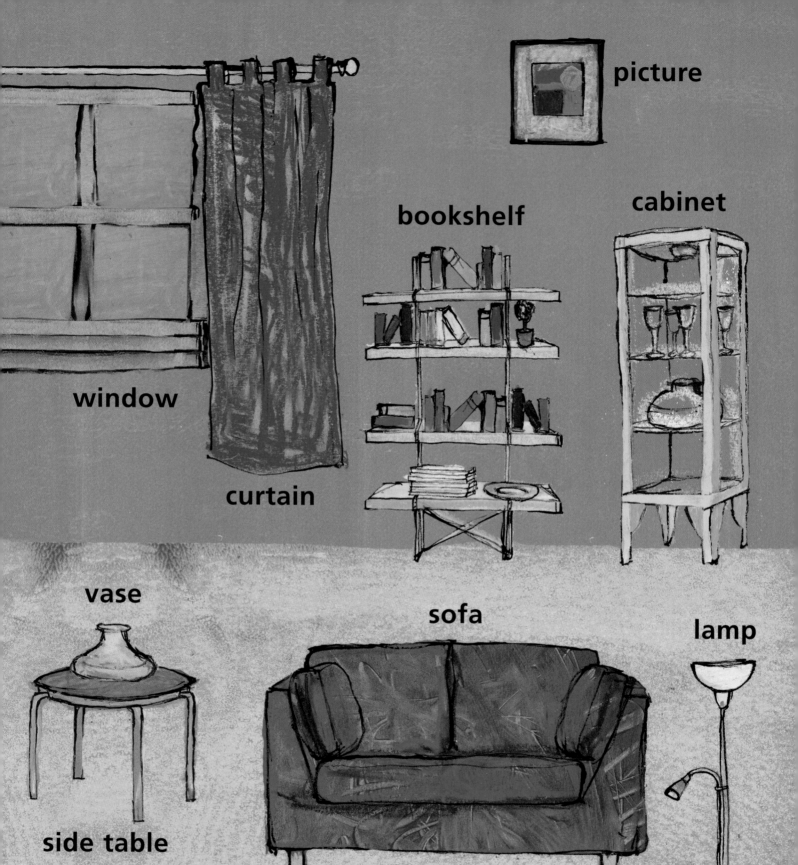

picture

bookshelf

cabinet

window

curtain

vase

sofa

lamp

side table

KITCHEN

bowl

glass

refrigerator

plate

napkin

teapot

cup

chair

table

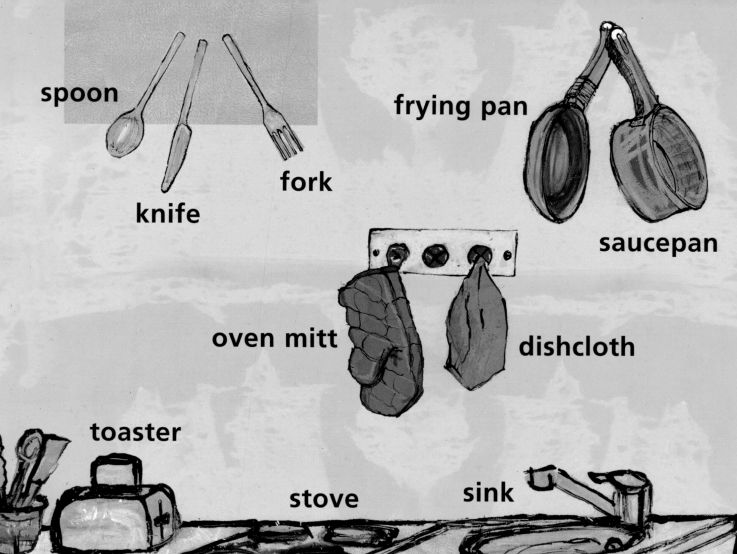

spoon

knife

fork

frying pan

saucepan

oven mitt

dishcloth

toaster

stove

sink

oven

VEGETABLES

potato

green bean

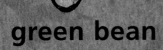

mushroom

carrot

asparagus

onion

pumpkin

peas

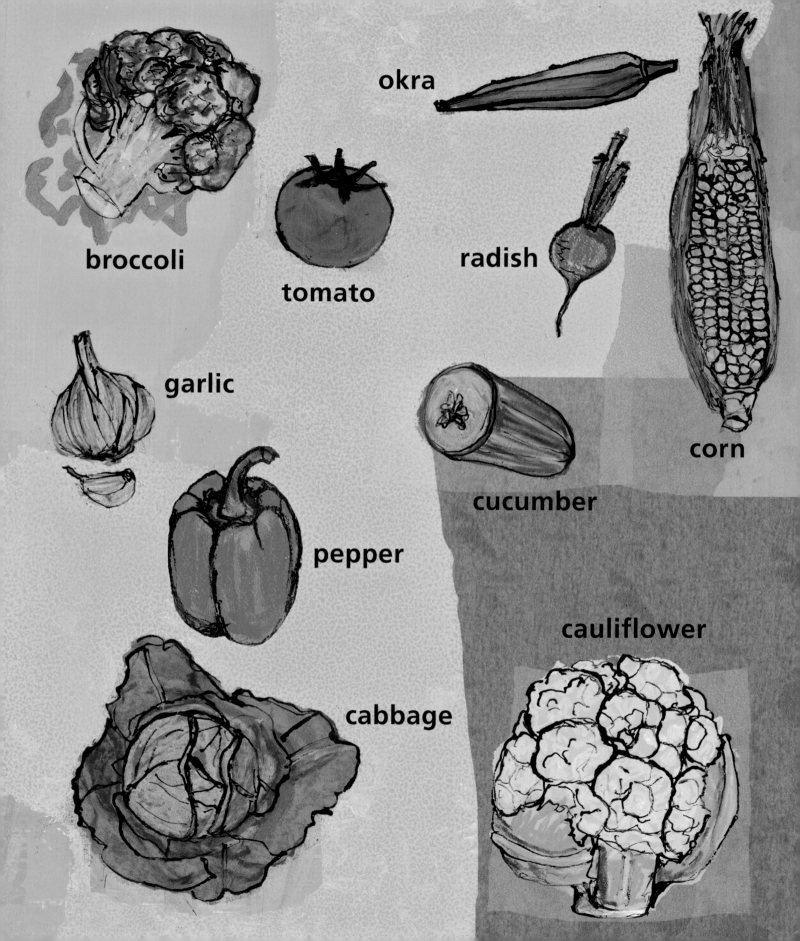

broccoli

okra

tomato

radish

corn

garlic

cucumber

pepper

cauliflower

cabbage

FOOD

sandwich

bread

cheese

milk

butter

honey

jam

egg

cereal

raisins

oil

fries

fruit juice

spaghetti

chocolate

cake

ice cream

BATHROOM

towel

mirror

sink

toilet paper

toilet

bathroom cabinet

potty

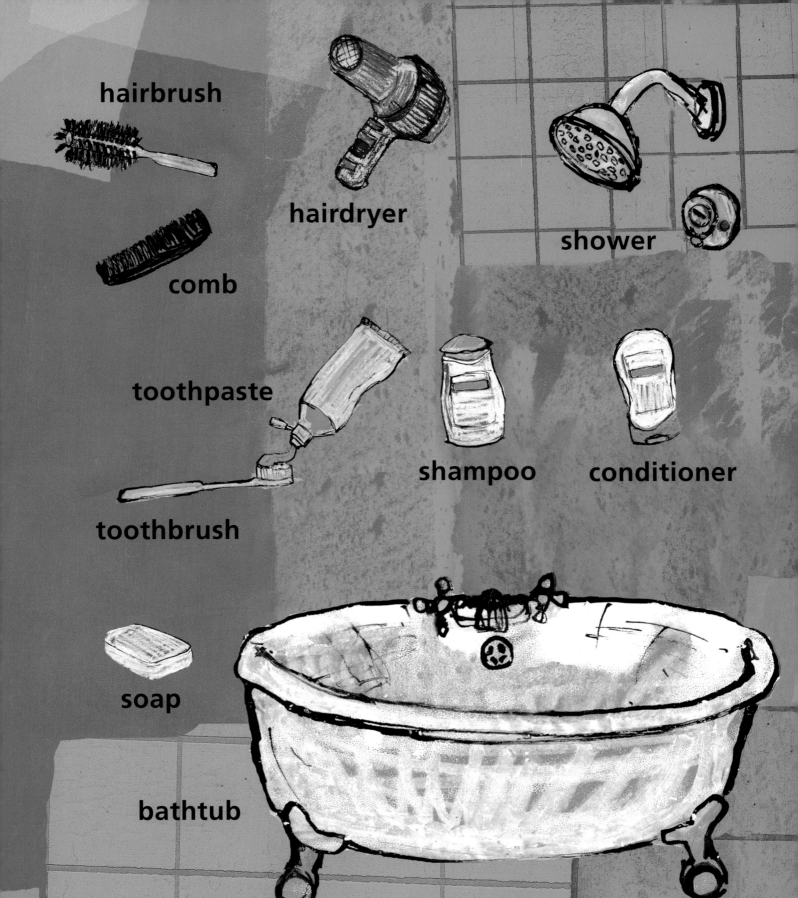

hairbrush

comb

hairdryer

shower

toothpaste

shampoo

conditioner

toothbrush

soap

bathtub

BEDROOM

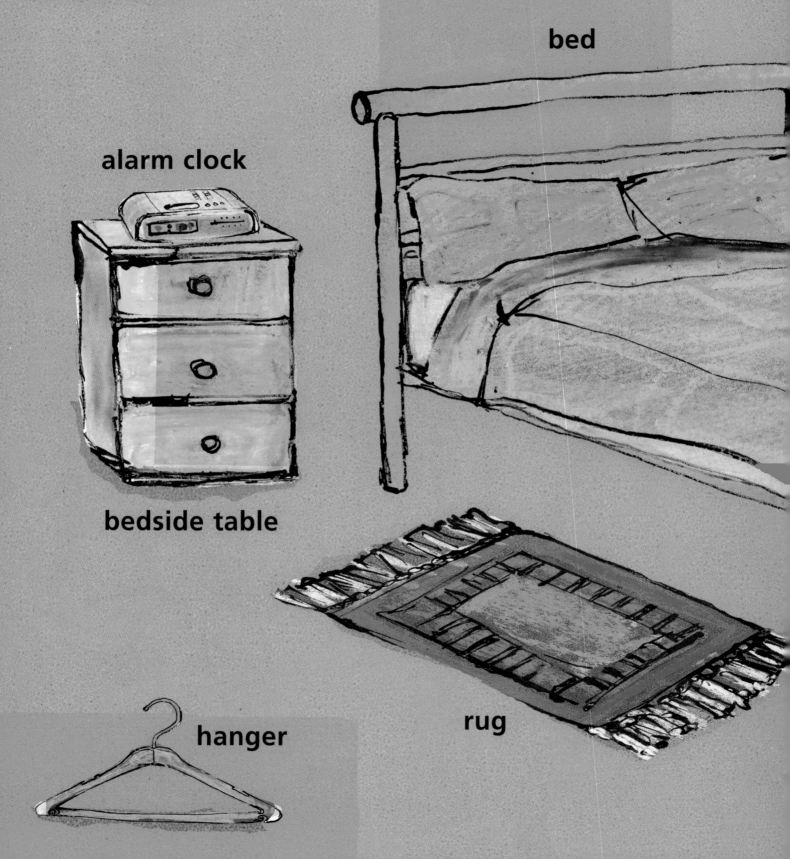

bed

alarm clock

bedside table

hanger

rug

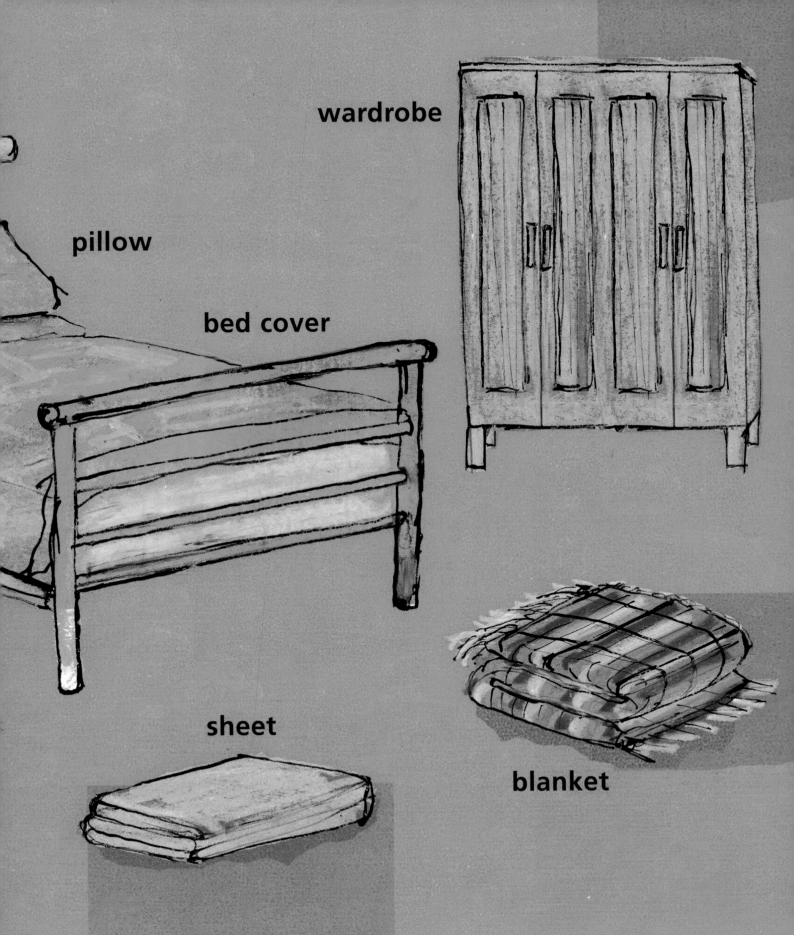

wardrobe

pillow

bed cover

sheet

blanket

CLOTHING

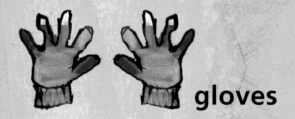
gloves

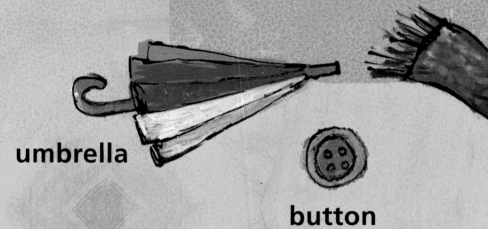
umbrella

button

T-shirt

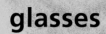
glasses

boxer shorts
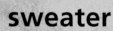

hat

underpants

sweater

jacket

slippers

scarf

backpack

skirt

shirt

handbag

socks

belt

jeans

pyjamas

shoes

shorts

COMMUNICATIONS

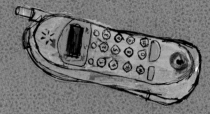

telephone

television

DVD player

video recorder

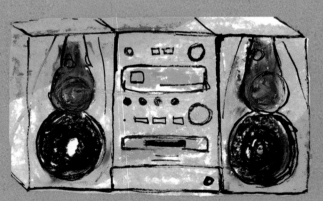

stereo

remote control

video camera

camera

TOOLS

screwdriver

screw

saw

stepladder

nail

drill

hammer

shovel

vacuum cleaner

paint

SCHOOL & OFFICE

pencil

marker

glue stick

book

stamp

ruler

pencil sharpener

pencil case

globe

crayon

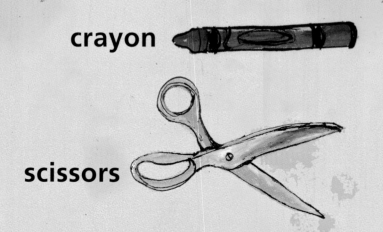

scissors

calculator

stapler

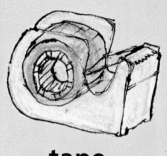

tape

paints

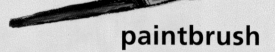

paintbrush

pen

envelope

computer

desk

notebook

NUMBERS

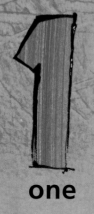
one

two

three

four

five

six

seven

eight

nine

ten

SHAPES

hexagon

rectangle

square

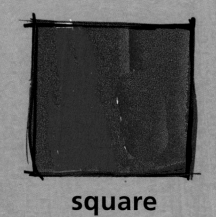

oval

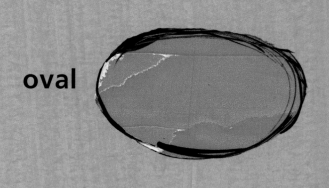

circle

triangle

octagon

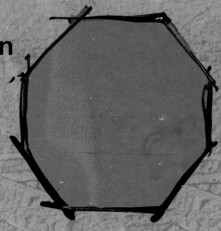

MUSICAL INSTRUMENTS

flute

guitar

violin

saxophone

bongos

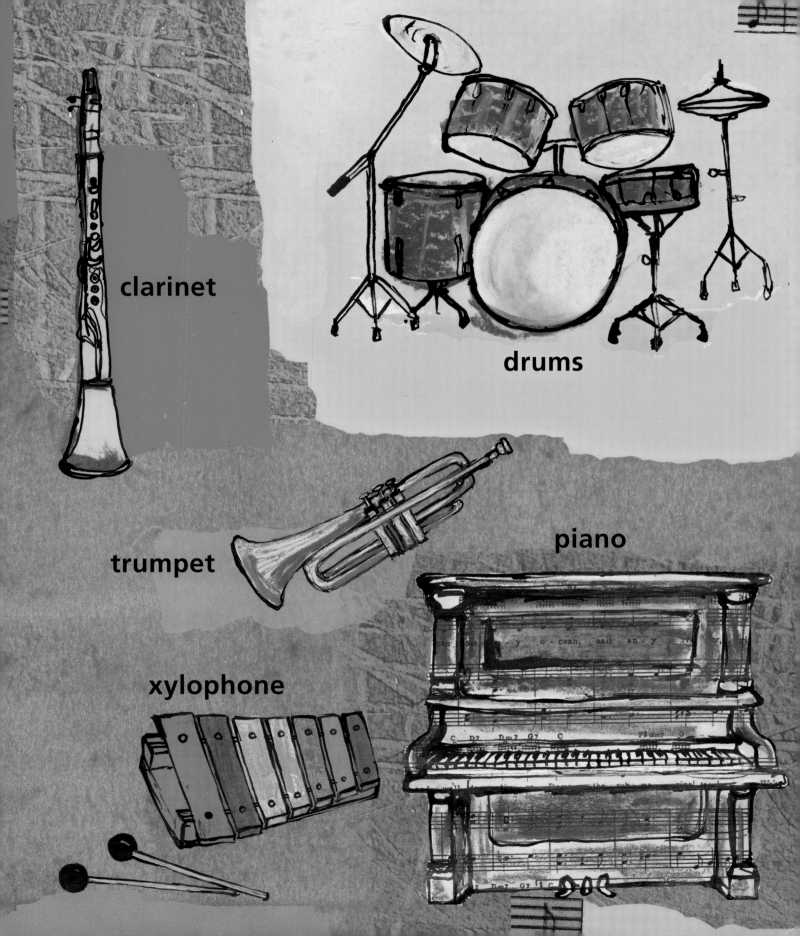

clarinet

drums

trumpet

piano

xylophone

SPORTS & GAMES

skateboard

video games

cards

football /
soccer ball

ice skates

rollerblades

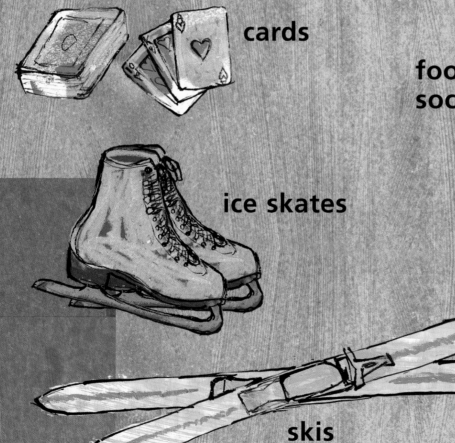

skis

chess

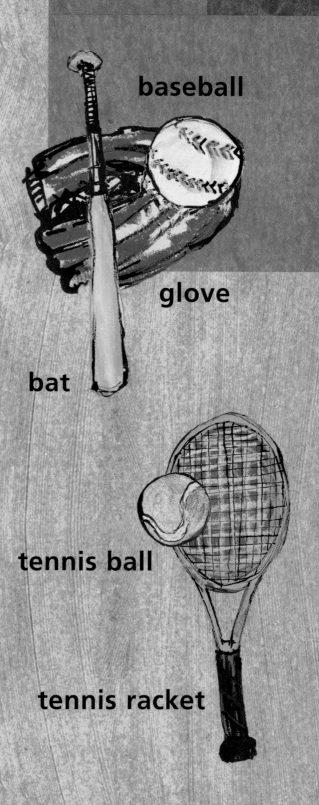
baseball

glove

bat

basketball

American football

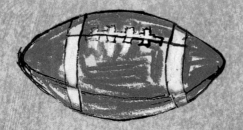

tennis ball

tennis racket

cricket ball

cricket bat

TRANSPORTATION

boat

bicycle

train

car

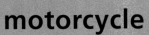
motorcycle

ambulance

helicopter

plane

fire engine

bus

truck

tractor

SEASIDE

ball

sky

beach towel

swimsuit

beach bag

sunglasses

sunscreen

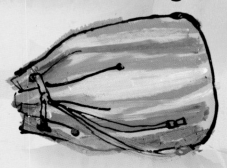

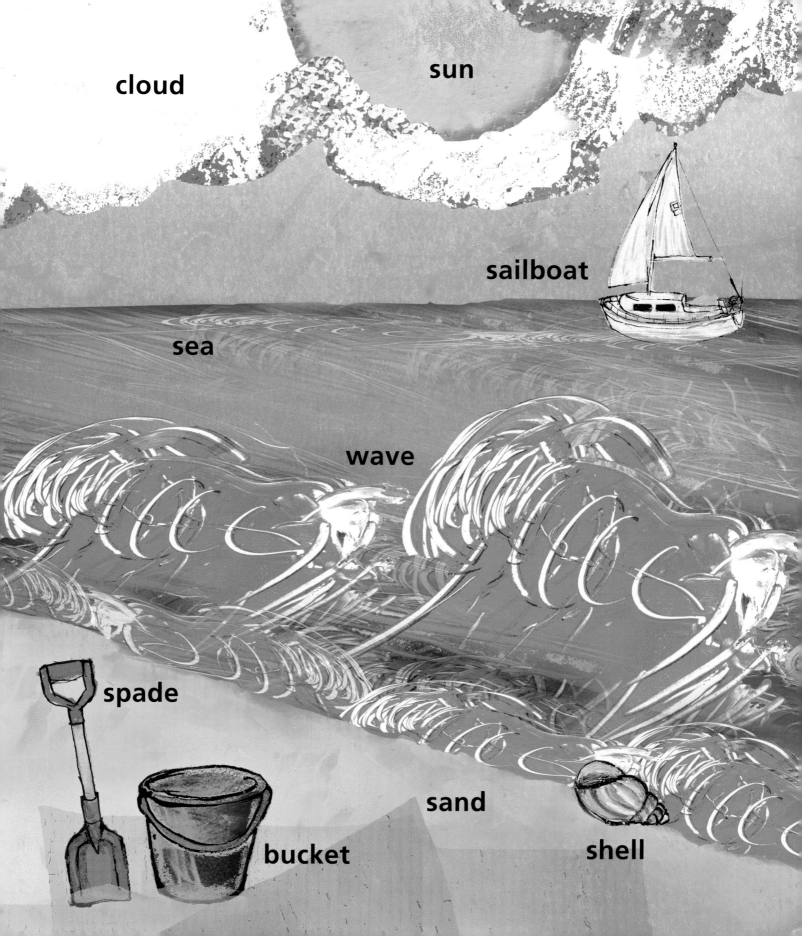

cloud

sun

sailboat

sea

wave

spade

sand

bucket

shell